PRINCIPLES OF LIFE

PRINCIPLES OF LIFE

Living in Victory

Bishop Travis Roberson

ELM HILL

A Division of
HarperCollins Christian Publishing

www.elmhillbooks.com

Principles of Life
Living in Victory

Published in Nashville, Tennessee, by Elm Hill, an imprint of Thomas Nelson. Elm Hill and Thomas Nelson are registered trademarks of HarperCollins Christian Publishing, Inc.

Elm Hill titles may be purchased in bulk for educational, business, fund-raising, or sales promotional use. For information, please e-mail SpecialMarkets@ThomasNelson.com.

Library of Congress Cataloging-in-Publication Data

Library of Congress Control Number: 2018939116

Prelaunch edition ISBN: 978-1-595558138

ISBN 978-1-595557391 (Paperback)
ISBN 978-1-595557469 (Hardbound)
ISBN 978-1-595557346 (eBook)

Principles of Life is dedicated to anyone who realizes that they need more structure in their life. These principles will help you identify and correct problem areas in ways that you will find not only practical, but also easy to use every day as well as being spiritually uplifting. In order for them to work, however, you must fully embrace them and choose to obey their directives. If you remain committed to these principles and steadfastly apply them to your personal situation even during difficult times, they will empower you to make the best possible life choices in any situation.

Foreword

I am humbled and thankful to have been chosen to create the Holy Temple of God and its "Principles of Life" outreach program. This program will help anyone who chooses to be loyal to its principles; the principles will strengthen you to make the best life choices in challenging situations. I was inspired to write this book while wrongly incarcerated for stealing motor fuel taxes. During my stay in prison, I witnessed the tragic revolving door of inmates released from prison returning only short weeks or months later for drug and alcohol offenses or other criminal misbehavior. Interviewing many of them revealed that inmates who were incarcerated for drug and alcohol-related crimes felt powerless when once again confronted with their drug of choice; these unfortunate individuals were soon repeating the same mistakes when difficult times crept into their lives and they could find no alternative coping mechanisms. They had no idea where to turn.

While I was incarcerated, I reflected on all my accomplishments and my blessings. First and foremost, I know I'm saved and sanctified and baptized with the Holy Ghost and with fire. God has blessed me with a loving wife and family. He has allowed me to retire from the military (US Air Force), earn my Aircraft Powerplant license from the Federal Aviation Administration; earn an associate's degree in Aircraft and Powerplant Technology, a bachelor's degree in Professional Aeronautics and a master's of Aeronautical Science; establish and operate a corporation, a limited liability company, and a nonprofit organization. Although I didn't feel blessed as I sat handcuffed and charged with theft, I cried out to the Lord for direction. He heard my cry and He strengthened me.

While locked up and waiting for sentencing, I personally studied the Bible from Genesis to Revelation many times. I also engaged in group Bible study and prayer on a daily basis with inmates who desired to know the Lord. Wanting to please the Lord by thanking Him for my safety and peace, I attended every available church service, worshipping and praising Him in Spirit and in truth. God moved in mighty ways and on many occasions, both personally and among those to whom I ministered.

Following the "Principles of Life" is a journey that must become your lifestyle. You must stay the course no matter what obstacles you encounter along the way. The benefits are immeasurable and everlasting. If you commit yourself to follow these principles no matter what, they will mold you into a person who will please God, a righteous man or woman who wholeheartedly loves the Lord. I'm confident that this book will be an invaluable resource for you, for your family, and for your community.

ACKNOWLEDGMENTS

This book is inspired by God. He strengthens me to trust Him with all my heart and not to depend on my understanding of this life. Everywhere He leads me I acknowledge Him as He directs my path. I also have many others to honor, praise, and thank.

First, I honor, praise, and thank my wife, Petrice. She loves the Lord and treats me well. God answers her prayers and protects her as she travels. God blesses her to always pray for me and satisfy my every desire and need. She's anointed as a public school administrator, as a Sunday school teacher, as a church group coordinator, as a mother, and as a grandmother. I also acknowledge her expertise in editing this book.

Next, I honor, praise, and thank my brother and sister-in-law, James and Nell Robinson. Out of the goodness of their hearts they cared for my wife, home, and property during the three-plus years I was incarcerated. They opened their home to my wife and gave her all the help and support she needed in my absence. They kept the grass cut each season; they cut up and burned an eighty-foot tall/four-foot diameter tree after God allowed it to fall away from our home during a severe storm; in the middle of the night they came out and secured a commercial building after a truck crashed through its walls. These are just a few examples of how God, in His goodness, allowed my brother to bless me in my absence.

Next I honor, praise, and thank my niece Lola Williams and her daughter Sharon. Though their income is limited, they sent funds to me that they could have used for themselves. They prepared meals for my wife many evenings so she didn't have to eat alone. They mailed loving, prayerful, and encouraging letters and cards regularly during my incarceration. I am truly blessed to have them in my life.

I also honor, praise, and thank John and Delouise Williams and family. They gave funds to post my bond and help secure my freedom. They also mailed loving and encouraging letters and cards that blessed my soul during the entire three-plus years of incarceration. We currently engage in weekly Bible study. They love the Lord and they bless my soul.

I also honor, praise, and thank my sister, Lela Brown. I believe she'd give her life for mine. She visited when she could during my incarceration and mailed loving and supportive letters and cards that blessed my soul.

I also honor, praise, and thank our accountant, Kathy Ballard Moses. She processed our business and personal taxes without charge during my incarceration. A true woman of God, she prayed "without ceasing" for my release and for my strength in the Lord. She has been a loyal friend and a stalwart supporter throughout our trials and tribulations.

Lastly, I honor, praise, and thank Paulette and Douglas Postell, MY LITTLE SISTER AND BROTHER. They truly love the Lord and me. They took the burden of driving to visit me from my wife on several occasions; they encouraged and supported my wife in my absence. During my incarceration, they sent funds and mailed loving cards and letters that blessed my soul.

All praise and honor to God for the great things He has done!

Travis Roberson

CONTENTS

INTRODUCTION

"Principles of Life" provides the tangible leadership and guidance you must use daily, especially when confronted with situations and circumstances that may tempt you to choose the "easy way out." The "easy way out" always leaves you vulnerable to grief, shame, hurt, and despair. This choice will always act like a boomerang, leading you back to the life you are trying to leave behind. These rules alone, however, do not cause you to obey the principles—you follow these principles because you trust God's Word. That is the key! This book is based entirely on God's Word. I speak from personal experience. These principles have become my lifestyle—and I am so very grateful that I was able to use them to strengthen me and deliver me from prison. They have blessed me to reach out to people everywhere.

The principles shared here are focus, humility, prayer, seeking God, repentance, forgiveness, and trusting and obeying God's Word. If you are loyal to these principles and let them guide your steps, you will change for the good and you'll be able to be trusted to do great things for the Lord. Remember, there is a difference between saved and unsaved, honesty and dishonesty, and repentance and lip service. I beg you not to fall into a trap, because that can happen so easily and when you least expect it. Thankfully, these principles will work for you if you work them.

Focus

Focus is the condition of being distinct, comprehensible, or clearly defined.

Focus is a distinct and clearly defined condition that one has, like a heart attack, virus or any other condition. However, unlike these common conditions, focus will not harm you at all; in fact, it is quite good for both your mental and spiritual health. The consequences of *not* having it, however, are very dangerous. In fact, if you don't have this condition, it will be difficult for you to stay on track with just about anything in your life.

The condition of being focused is all about our ability to properly understand the world around us, as well as our inner lives. For example, consider your body. When you eat nourishing foods and exercise, your body will have the best chance to function with optimum performance and to be and to remain healthy. Likewise, if we nourish our minds and hearts with positive studies and spiritual nourishments, we'll have good, pleasant, and refreshing attitudes. By contrast, if we don't eat properly and instead eat (or overeat!) a lot of junk food and / or smoke or engage in other bad habits such as alcohol or drugs, we are in effect sabotaging our health. Not only do we risk becoming obese and far more susceptible to all kinds of preventable and potentially fatal diseases such as diabetes, cancer and heart disease, but we also can't concentrate well because we become weak and nauseated, and our minds are just not right.

Now think how different that scenario would be if you were instead disciplined—and focused—enough to eat a healthy diet and sleep eight hours daily. The results would likely be amazing: you would almost certainly achieve better grades in school and perform more proficiently on the job. Add exercise to your routine and the improvements will soon soar off the chart. You don't have to become a "health nut" or a bodybuilder, just a highly focused individual who knows the importance of setting goals with a dogged determination not to veer away from them. Don't worry, this new frame of mind gets easier with practice. You learned to focus on things that were bad for you and dragging you down, so now it's time to focus on the many things that are good for you and will lift you up.

Moreover, make no mistake about it: this principle applies every bit as much to your spiritual life. Just as these eating and lifestyle regimens improve your physical condition, studying and obeying the Word of God can work wonders on your focus, too. It will help you to develop a positive attitude even though people around you are doing you wrong. Think about that for a minute. Imagine how different your outlook on just about everything would be if you focused your mind and your attention on the things of God, rather than solely on the things of the world. As Holy Scripture tells us, we are to live in this world while at the same time not becoming part of it. We should live as ambassadors for Christ passing through this world to spread the Good News, but our real and permanent citizenship is in the eternal

Kingdom of God. This is a very important point, because the Bible clearly spells out a sharply distinct contrast between the "carnal" man and a Spirit-filled Christian.

Getting to heaven is not about how others treat you, but getting there is about loving God and His people. He says in His word, "How you can say you love me if you don't obey Me" John 14:15 (KJV). It's a profound question. Many people claim to love God, but then go and live a life that is completely dishonoring to Him and antithetical to everything He has taught us. If we are foolish enough to live that way, we are doing tremendous damage to our own souls, because disobeying God is, to say the least, not a very good way of showing how much we love Him. In fact, it makes our claims to "love" God seem like nothing but a bunch of hot air.

Now, I realize that only God truly knows what is in a man's (or woman's) heart, and He knows we are all sinners who stumble from time to time. But that is where _focus_ comes in! Try making obeying God's commands the centerpiece and focus of your life, and His Word your moral compass. That will keep you safely on the hallowed "narrow path" that the Bible promises us leads to eternal life.

Another scripture puts it this way: "No one has ever seen God; but if we love one another, God lives in us and his love is made complete in us" I John 4:12 (NIV). Wow, this is God confronting us with a reality that we simply cannot deny. Sure while living on this earth we don't see God face to face. No, but we sure do see plenty of other people every day, don't we? And remember you, me, and every person who ever lived was created by God, and in the image of God. That is why God equates loving other people with loving God Himself. No wonder Jesus said that whatever we do (for either good or bad) to the least of

3

His brethren, we have done it to Him. The next time you interact with another human being, try to keep in mind, how you would treat Almighty God in that situation ... and then be sure to treat that fellow human being accordingly.

Therefore, it is not about how others treat you that enables you to get to heaven, but it is about how you treat others that gets you there. So, how are you going to know how to treat others unless you are taught what it is that you must do? This is why studying is so important, more especially the Word of God. He says in His Word to study to "show yourself approved by God, a workman that might not be ashamed, but rightly divide the word of truth" 2 Timothy 3:16 (KJV). Talk about focused! What is being described here is a person who knows how to concentrate (focus) his or her attention in the right direction, which is on the spiritual aspects of life as taught to us in the Bible. And once you know the Word, you must then follow through and live out its precepts to the best of your abilities in your daily life. As the saying goes: "They will know we are Christians by how they see us love one another." That's right, an important facet of witnessing for the Lord and spreading His Gospel is to let the world see that your love is genuine—for God, for your neighbors, and even for your enemies. The more focused you are, the more others will come to appreciate the power of true "agape" love as consistently practiced by a dedicated Christian. This will help open the gates of heaven not only for yourself, but also for others too. Remember, more than once Jesus described the Kingdom of God as a great banquet feast, and our Father's will is for all to attend.

When God gives you visions, missions, and instructions, don't focus on the nouns that make it seem impossible to achieve, but focus on the distinct, clearly defined actions He wants you to perform. Allow the Spirit of God to lead, guide, and help achieve His visions and missions. Don't depend on self or anyone else to define God's distinct, comprehensible, or clearly defined plans that He has given you. We lose focus by allowing our minds and hearts to be led away from what is distinct, comprehensible, or clearly defined. For example, if we know that two plus two is four, why try another answer? If we know that exercise and a healthy diet sustain a healthy body, why do something contrary? And if we know that studying the Bible and earning degrees will improve our ability to serve others and God, we should focus our time and abilities on that goal.

Yes, God wants men and women who are "on fire" for Him and ready to change the world. The apostles and the disciples of the early Church lived out their faith with boundless passion, zeal and commitment, and God bestowed great power upon them on the day of Pentecost. And He will do the same for us! Why? Because when we focus on God, He comes to us and moves in our lives in miraculous and often unexpected ways. No wonder the Bible says that He is "in our midst" when two or more gather "in His Name." What does it mean to "gather in His Name?" It means that people are joining their hearts and minds for the single—i.e., focused—purpose of worshipping the Lord. God really loves it when we do that. He knows that it unifies us in common purpose. It cements a community of faith that loves God, loves one another, and then reaches out beyond their own church community to be "salt and light" to the world at large. There is no limit to what one highly focused Christian can accomplish, so just think how much God-given power there is when they join forces, and *focus* their energy on being a powerful force in the world.

When it comes to focus, it is one of the simplest of the

principles that we will be learning about, but also one of the most profound. We can rest assured that if we study the Word of God and allow Him to guide us, He will allow us to be with Him forever. This thought alone should keep us focused on both His warnings and on His promises.

HUMILITY

Humility is an honest expression of meekness and submission to God. Anything else is counterfeit. Scripture tells us that only the things we do for God will last. So we must be sure we're humbling ourselves before God. All our blessings flow from positioning ourselves in humility.

This makes so much sense when you prayerfully think about it. How can we not feel humility when we contemplate the might, majesty, and holy perfection of God? Oftentimes, especially these days, people approach God far too casually, without giving the due reverence that is due to Him as Creator and sovereign Ruler of the entire universe.

Of course, it was not always this way. Back in the Old Testament, for example, when Moses encountered God's presence upon seeing the burning bush, he immediately removed his shoes, for he was now standing on "holy ground." This was indeed an act of great humility for Moses, as it signified that he was accepting God as His Lord and Savior, and he, Moses, was humbly at His service.

An even more powerful depiction of God's holiness comes

to us from the prophet Isaiah. At the inception of his prophetic career, Isaiah received a stunning vision from God:

> **In the year that king Uzziah died I saw also the Lord sitting upon a throne, high and lifted up, and his train filled the temple. Above it stood the seraphims: each one had six wings; with twain he covered his face, and with twain he covered his feet, and with twain he did fly.**
>
> **And one cried unto another, and said, Holy, holy, holy, *is* the LORD of hosts: the whole earth *is* full of his glory.**
>
> **And the posts of the door moved at the voice of him that cried, and the house was filled with smoke.**
>
> **Then said I, Woe *is* me! for I am undone; because I *am* a man of unclean lips, and I dwell in the midst of a people of unclean lips: for mine eyes have seen the King, the LORD of hosts.**
>
> **Then flew one of the seraphims unto me, having a live coal in his hand, *which* he had taken with the tongs from off the altar: And he laid *it* upon my mouth, and said, Lo, this hath touched thy lips; and thine iniquity is taken away, and thy sin purged**
>
> Isaiah 6: 1–7 (KJV).

What was God's purpose in unveiling this dramatic scene? These verses are so rich with profound lessons. The Lord wanted to show the prophet—and through him all the people, including us—just who exactly they (we) are dealing with when calling upon God. He is called "Holy" by the heavenly creatures around His throne three times, a sign of perfection (and a reflection of the Trinity as well) that lets us know that when we come to Him in prayer, humility is absolutely the only acceptable attitude. If we give deference and loyalty to earthly rulers, how much more do we owe our most ultimate humility to the King of Kings and Lord of Lords?

In fact, Isaiah's humility upon seeing, firsthand, God's unequalled majesty and holiness, is so intense that he is overcome with feelings of sinfulness and inadequacy. But God immediately makes it clear that He rewards the prophet for his proper understanding of his position before God. He provides a way for Isaiah to be cleansed of his sins and made worthy of proclaiming God's messages to the people. From that point on, he became one of the most respected prophets in all the land of Israel.

Submission and humility extends to how we interact with our fellow human beings as well. It means being subject to or accountable to another person, and meekness is patience and submission. Consider this: without humility, there is no accountability or patience. Humility is much more important than most people realize. It is one of the first and foremost elements that God requires of you in order to make you whole. What's so wonderful about God's Word is that it's true and beneficial whether you believe it or not. As you seek His will through His Word, He will build your faith and your priorities will change because you will want to please Him in all that you do.

Of course, even the simple act of seeking God's will through His Word requires humility. It means accepting that whatever God tells us is correct—it is the best way. If it contradicts something that we ourselves believe, then we have a choice: either believe our own thoughts or believe what God is clearly telling us. Choosing God means choosing the path of humility. That is the path of holy obedience, regardless of how difficult that road may be.

Let me share with you a little bit of my own experience with this topic.

God blessed me with a degree of humility from an early age. But I would allow people to take advantage of my kindness when they mistook it for weakness. There always seemed to be some folks who would borrow things and wouldn't return them. Others would assign me their responsibilities and take credit for my work. Some would lie and misrepresent what I said and did. Many would come in the name of the Lord, but would say things that simply weren't true. And still others would steal vital resources from me that were painfully needed elsewhere.

Does any of this sound familiar? If you find yourself in similar circumstances, do not react with anger. Being humble and following Christ *does* mean holding your tongue sometimes, and having great patience. However, it *does not* mean you have to allow yourself to be treated like a doormat. All human beings, humble or not, deserve respect and to be treated with courtesy, so you also need to know when to stand up for yourself, and for others who are not being treated fairly. Remember we are all made in the image of God, therefore from our very conception we are due human dignity and human rights. This is a rule with no exceptions.

Getting back to my own story: although I endured these trials with feelings of hurt, grief, and pain, it was while incarcerated that I most keenly learned the power of meekness and submission. God sat me down and gave me a good understanding of His Word and will for me. After studying the scriptures from Genesis to Revelation with pen and paper in hand, He gave me an understanding and a vision for what I must do for the rest of my life here on earth.

And, yes, all of this happened while in the harsh environment of living behind the bleak walls of a prison. Godly power gave me peace in the middle of my troubles. If you want peace, ask God—then expect to receive what you ask. Cast all doubt from your heart and mind, and pray with great expectations. Do not be presumptuous about the answers—it is up to God to do as He see fits—but your duty is to know with one hundred percent certainty that whatever God decides to do, ultimately it is in your best interest and will bring great Glory to God. As we read in Romans...

And we know that all things work together for good to them that love God, to them who are the called according to his purpose

ROMANS 8:28 (KJV).

Pray in faith for the power of the Holy Ghost. Peace is only one element of the power of the Holy Spirit that He will give you. Keep asking until you get it! Persistence is of paramount importance. Now mind you, I'm not talking about "things" but about Godly blessings. Remember to thank God for His blessings. The Bible tells us that we are to show thanksgiving in everything we do. Moreover, we show Him love when we obey Him. Jesus said, "If you love me, keep my commandments"

JOHN 14:15 (KJV).

I exercised meekness and submission when I went about everything that I did with great patience, and with a humble attitude toward those appointed over me and, especially, toward God. I was told when I could go to the commissary, when I could go to church, when I could go to Bible study, when to bathe, brush my teeth, eat, and change my underwear, as just a few examples of how humble God enabled me to become. It was, to be sure, not always easy and not always pleasant. But because of my humility, our merciful God has blessed me even more. I learned a life-changing lesson while in prison. The message was if I could be this humble to God's creation, then I must be even more humble to God's Word. Humbling yourself to your fellow human beings, as Jesus taught through His own example, builds you up so that you are spiritually strong enough to take God's Word into your heart and know how to put yourself second, with God always out in front of you leading the way.

Patience and Accountability

Living God's Word enables me to live in peace while labeled a thief, a criminal, an alcoholic, and a drug addict even though the circumstances behind all of these are far from what anyone could call fair. The company had proper documentation showing its authorization to operate in the manner it did prior to my arrest, so the charges were bogus in the first place. Nonetheless, caught up in the oftentimes misnamed "justice" system, I had to follow all of the rules and restrictions as though I were in fact guilty.

They certainly weren't going to make it easy. According to parole release stipulations, I was ordered to attend Alcoholic Anonymous (AA) meetings, report to a parole officer monthly, pay personal funds for restitution for a limited liability company (LLC) debt, and obtain prior approval to travel to any destination outside the state. Imagine yourself in similar circumstances. Put yourself in my shoes for a moment—how would you react?

Yes, I could have become bitter and angry over all the injustice … but my Father in heaven had other plans.

God allowed me to stand this test to glorify Him in the midst of my trials. With the power of God, I am diligently and patiently obeying these stipulations as unto the Lord. This has also provided me with a tremendous opportunity to reach out to any of His people who are willing to humble themselves in order to break their addictions and live like God wants them to live. If it were not for the long ordeal I had to endure, my witness for other hurting people would have never been as strong. It all has made me realize the profound truth behind the scripture that says: "If we are distressed, it is for your comfort and salvation; if we are comforted, it is for your comfort, which produces in you patient endurance of the same sufferings we suffer" 2 Corinthians 1:6 (NIV). Like Paul, because of what I personally went through, my testimony of endurance could touch suffering people directly in their hearts as they undergo their own trials.

I'm grateful for being delivered from prison. Attending AA meetings allowed me to witness firsthand how His people struggle on their own to stay free from drugs and alcohol. They bond, fellowship, and deliver powerful testimonies on how they take one day at a time in battling their addictions. Some say they have prayed and that God has taken the taste of drugs from them, yet they still call themselves "addicts." This is why trusting that if you "confess with your mouth that Jesus is Lord and believe in your heart that God raised Him from the dead you shall be saved" Romans 10:9 (NIV) is so important.

If you believe this Word you will also believe that when you pray for deliverance and God answers your prayer, you're free from that sin. Sure, the thought will return because the sinful nature still lives inside of us who are free from sin. But we don't obey its urges because we know its source. It comes from the evil one and not from God. You are no longer a slave to the addiction. God says I will be judged for everything I think and do in my body, and, since He's the one who has the power to destroy sinful bodies and souls, I'm committed to His word.

After all, doesn't that only make sense, since it is He Who created us in the first place? Just like an inventor understands his invention better than anyone else, our Creator knows us inside and out better than we even know ourselves! If He says something is wrong, it is wrong. Likewise, if He says we are forgiven of something and it no longer has a hold on our lives, believe that beautiful truth completely and with all your heart. That is the best way to make absolutely certain that you don't backslide into those same old bad patterns and habits again and again. Actually, getting out of prison is a good analogy for this. Once you are no longer behind bars, why create imaginary bars in your mind? Believe what God says about freedom from sin: "Then you will know the truth, and the truth will set you free" John 8:32 (NIV).

Now I'm thankful for my trials because He has empowered me as I journeyed through all of them. He has convinced me that to be absent from my body is to be present with Him so long as I live according to His will until I die. Therefore, I trust His promise that the glory He'll give me in the end, whose greatness no one can perceive, will be my reward for going through the trials I experience in this life. As a matter of fact, the Bible teaches us this important lesson about suffering:

"I consider that our present sufferings are not worth comparing with the glory that will be revealed in us"
ROMANS 8:18 (NIV).

By the way, Apostle Paul had himself faced more trials and sufferings in his life than most of us ever will—shipwrecks, beatings, imprisonment—so clearly this was a man who knew exactly what he was talking about and was speaking from experience. Yet, through it all his trust and faith in God never wavered.

The underlying message here is to choose humility. Operating in humility causes you to be accountable to God for everything you think and do. It gives you the patience to know that your problems are temporary and will soon pass away. Did not our Lord and Savior Jesus Christ teach this very same lesson? "I have told you these things, so that in me you may have peace. In this world you will have trouble. But take heart! I have overcome the world" John 16:33 (NIV).

Wow! I know that I can really relate to those words; how about you? Do you see how Jesus does not promise that we will be trouble-free in this world? Yes, difficulties and obstacles will be with us throughout our natural lives, but He does promise that He has *overcome* the world, meaning that you can have His peace (a peace which "surpasses all understanding") right here and right now, all the while looking forward to spending all eternity with Him and all the redeemed, in God's kingdom where all troubles, sorrows and hardships have been banished forever.

Above all, I don't want you to become discouraged. When you have a negative feeling, you need to talk to someone. Make that someone God. This brings us to the second principle you need in order to be made whole. This principle is prayer.

PRAYER

Prayer is simply talking to God. When you pray, it's important to expect that your prayer will be answered. Equally important is to show that you trust God will answer your prayer by living as if your prayer has already been answered. When you believe God you trust Him, and that pleases Him. You are His friend and you are counted righteous and justified by faith. If what you're asking for is best for you and you're praying according to His will, your prayer will be answered. But if you're praying for something that's not good for you and is out of God's will, He will not answer your prayer. Well, at least not in the way you were hoping for Him to answer it. Therefore, it's very important to be in tune with God's will and to seek discernment regarding your heart's desire. Never can there be any substitute for lining up your will with the perfect holy will of God. In fact, that is the basis for a successful prayer life: make it God-centered … not me-centered.

God answers prayers based on His will. God's will for us is to prosper and be in good health even as our soul prospers. When we're filled with the Holy Spirit and we don't know what to pray for, the Holy Spirit prays for us and God answers His prayer.

I'm not talking about worldly possessions. I'm talking about the good and perfect gifts, the spiritual ones that only He provides. That is why it's so important to be humble when talking to God because you know you are not worthy of anything for which you're asking Him. You need patience enough to wait until He gives you what you're asking for, because He is doing so entirely out of grace not out of any obligation on His part. Moreover, it is imperative for you to be patient enough to trust that God didn't answer your prayer because what you asked for wasn't best for you. You must be accountable enough to know where you are with God. Are you operating in sin or in righteousness justified by faith and works? He sometimes says "Yes," sometimes "No," and sometimes "Wait." As you operate in humility, you'll understand what to pray for and you will always acknowledge that the answer must be according to His will.

Take a moment to think about the nature of humility and why it is so important when it comes to your relationship with God. First and foremost, it puts everything into its proper perspective. He is the Creator and you are the creature. The Bible uses the analogy of a potter making something from clay, which is particularly appropriate since, according to scripture, our bodies were made from the "dust of the earth" and then God breathed into Adam, the first man, and he became a living soul. Therefore, we owe our entire existence to God, and we rely upon Him for literally every breath that we take. So, in humility, we must always be mindful that the Creator knows exactly what He is doing. God is omnipotent, and He knows what we, His creations, need far better than we ourselves can ever know. He wrote the "owner's manual" for human life—the Holy Bible— and our duty is to read it so that we know how our Creator wants us to live.

I know that takes a lot of humility, and humility is simply not a part of our fallen nature. In fact, pride, the opposite of humility, played a huge role in the Fall of man, and it continues to make human beings act in ways contrary to God's will. It makes us think we don't really need Him. Thanks, but no thanks, God, I can take care of this myself. No wonder the Bible says, "Pride goes before a fall." Without humility, your prayer life will be destined for failure, as you are left wondering, *Why isn't God listening to me?* The problem is you're asking the wrong question. What you should be asking is, *Why I aren't I listening to God?* Here's a clue: swallow your pride and acknowledge that God's ways are always "higher" than our own, which is why we can never go wrong when we resolve to humbly follow Him.

OK, now we'll discuss here how to pray and when to pray.

How to Pray

Scripture says that we must pray by calling out to the Father in heaven. The Lord's Prayer, which Jesus Himself explicitly taught to us at the Sermon on the Mount, is the ideal formula for all prayer. We don't necessarily need to use its exact words; however, it is always advisable to use the concepts of the Lord's Prayer as the framework for all prayer.

Let's look at it step by step.

Our Father, who art in heaven, hallowed be thy name. We must understand to Whom we're calling. Our prayers are not being directed to "the universe": we address God personally, calling Him, as Jesus instructed, "Our Father." He is the Creator God who made the heavens, earth, and everything for us. Therefore we must never be more loyal to anyone or anything than we are to our Creator. We must honor Him with our hearts, our minds, our families, and our possessions while we praise Him for who He is and for all that He does for us, putting Him first in our lives.

Notice the form of address that we are told to use. It is on the one hand very personal, calling God "Our Father," yet, at the same time, His name is to be uttered with the utmost reverence. First, we acknowledge that He is our Heavenly Father, elevating Him above all others. And when we say, "hallowed be thy name," we are praising God for His holiness, meaning that His name must always be used only with the greatest possible respect.

Thy kingdom come, thy will be done, on earth as it is in heaven. God's will on earth and in heaven is perfect. There is no sin in His will or in heaven. There is no pain, crying or dying, just to name a few. This is also said in order to demonstrate God's sovereignty, as well as His omnipotence and omnipresence. He is everywhere all at once, and His Kingship extends to all creation. Nothing is beyond the Lord's rule. His Word is the final word, and His will ultimately prevails in all things, all in God's perfect timing.

Give us this day our daily bread. This means that we know that God will provide everything that we need every day. Do you take your "daily bread" for granted? None of us ever should! The only reason we have anything at all—including life itself—is because the Lord so graciously granted it to us. He did not have to give us anything … but He gives us everything because He is a cheerful giver (just as He admonishes us to be in the Bible). It pleases God when we acknowledge that we are totally dependent on Him. It shows how grateful we are and how trusting when we place all our faith in Him. People may let you down. God never will.

And forgive us our trespasses as we forgive those who trespass against us. There is freedom in forgiving. Unforgiveness causes you excess stress. Your body deteriorates under stress and is unable to function as intended; it is sinning against God when you don't forgive. Now you'll have to shamefully ask God for "forgiveness for your unforgiveness" so you can get back into a right relationship with Him. Remember that anything we've thought or done against God's will is sin. All of that must be cleaned out of our bodies, God's temple, if we want to remain justified as righteous with God. How can we expect God to forgive us when we refuse to forgive our fellow human beings? Think of the parable that Jesus told about the unforgiving servant (Matthew 18:21–35). Read it and realize why we have no right to be unforgiving. Instead, we need to obey God and drop all our grudges right now. Vendettas and plotting vengeance has no place in the life of a Christian. As we read in Psalm 37:8, "Calm your anger and abandon wrath. Don't be angry—it only leads to evil."

And lead us not into temptation. This a very scary area. Scripture says that God doesn't tempt us with evil. I haven't heard a clarification that I can wrap my mind around to explain what this means. I know He hardened Pharaoh's heart so that Pharaoh would not obey Him so that the children of Egypt would come to know Him. So I fear Him enough to obey Him; I recommend you do the same. Perhaps one way to think about it is this: not only will God not lead us into temptation, but he will lead us *away* from temptation. Consider, for example, I Corinthians 10:13, where we read: "No temptation has overtaken you except what is common to mankind. And God is faithful; he will not let you be tempted beyond what you can bear. But when you are tempted, he will also provide a way out so that you can endure it." This passage should make us very thankful that our Father is such a merciful God.

But deliver us from evil. Evil is sin. Anything you do against God's word or will is evil. God says be ye perfect as your Father in heaven is perfect. God gave us the power to act, faith to trust Him, His word of truth and key to eternal life, the power to choose right from wrong and the power of the Holy Spirit to counsel, lead, and guide us. He gave us all we need to live a life He demands. Again, God's word is true whether one believe it or not. He wants you to believe, obey, and be saved. There is only one way to be "delivered from evil" and that is by Jesus Christ. That is why He is called our Lord and Savior. He is the one who defeats evil, thereby protecting us and freeing us from sin and all its evil consequences.

For thine is the Kingdom, the power, and the Glory forever. The whole duty of man is to worship God. You are worshiping God when you honor or value Him. You are honoring Him in your worship as you recognize His position as the Kingdom, the power, and the glory. He is the Kingdom because He has the authority to decree and enforce His sovereign rules. He is the power because He is omnipotent, meaning He can do all things. He is the Glory because His weighty importance and shining majesty accompany Him always and in every circumstance. The scripture says that if we endure these trials until the end, the glory He will give us in the end will be our reward. We'll have bodies just like Jesus' except for the crucifixion scars from His passion.

The scriptures also tell us that sometimes you must fast and pray in order for God to do certain works. One of these works is casting out demons. When you pray and it's not answered, try fasting and praying. An incident that happened to the apostles comes to mind. *Then the disciples came to Jesus privately and said, "Why could we not cast it out?" So, Jesus said to them,*

"Because of your unbelief; for assuredly, I say to you, if you have faith as a mustard seed, you will say to this mountain, 'Move from here to there, and it will move; and nothing will be impossible for you. However, this kind does not go out except by prayer and fasting." Matthew 17:19–21(NKJV).

And if it's still not answered, just acknowledge that God knows best and simply worship Him.

When to Pray

The Bible makes it very clear that we must pray continually. In I Thessalonians we read: *Rejoice evermore. Pray without ceasing. In every thing give thanks: for this is the will of God in Christ Jesus concerning you* I Thessalonians 5:16-18 (KJV). Notice how never-ending rejoicing and thanking God for everything go right along with ceaseless praying? So if you want to be happy all the time, there is the key … be ever thankful for all that God has given you, and never stop praying!

Indeed, we must pray as we go along our daily activities. We can do all good things and pray. When one does sinful things and is going through the motion of praying, he is playing with his life. Why? Because God has already come as our Savior! And we do not know when He will return. And when He returns, He's coming as our Judge. At that point it will be too late to repent. We will be judged for everything we've thought and done in our bodies. That is why it's so vitally important to continually pray that we are forgiven for things we have thought and done that didn't please Him. The scripture says that the righteous, we who are justified by faith, will scarcely get into heaven. There will be no hope for those who do sinful things and refuse to repent to enter into heaven. We must pray for the power of the Holy Spirit that helps us do great works. The Holy Ghost enables us to comply with God's Law.

With the awesome and powerful wise leadership and guidance of the Holy Spirit, we're empowered to love which covers a multitude of sins; and we cease to be lawbreakers. We turn our hearts over to God without reservation and He continues in His unconditional love for us, which He pours out freely, simply because it is His holy nature to be magnanimous and graceful, which is why He will respond with amazing mercy to all who call upon His name. For, as the Bible teaches, "Nor is there salvation in any other, for there is no other name under heaven given among men by which we must be saved" Acts 4:12 (NKJV).

SEEK GOD

To seek God, you must honestly hear, study, and question His word to understand and obey it. Judge yourself whether or not you are truly and fully seeking Him. Ask God for the power to understand, obey, and do His word so you may please Him in everything you do. Always remember seeking God requires courage, discipline, honesty, respect, responsibility, and tolerance. You must use all these principles as you genuinely search for God.

There are so many benefits that we derive from seeking God. As we diligently yearn for God, it is only natural that we will certainly grow in our knowledge of Him. In Acts 17:27 (NKJV) we read: "That they should seek God, and perhaps feel their way toward him and find him. Yet he is actually not far from each one of us." What a remarkable passage! First, it implores us to indeed seek God, to "feel" our way toward Him. In other words, your entire life should be impacted by this "search" for God; by "feeling" your way toward God, you are listening for His voice and seeking to follow Him wherever He leads you. The passage ends with an assurance that God is in fact "not far from each one of us." The implication, of course, is that if we steadfastly seek Him, we will no doubt find Him.

Do we want to live as Godly men, women, boys and girls? If so, the only way is to be earnest and sincere in our quest. Interesting enough, as we seek Him, He has already been seeking us. Consider the words of Psalm 14:2 (KJV)... "The LORD has looked down from heaven upon the sons of men, To see if there are any who understand, Who seek after God." Therefore, the very act of seeking God is in and of itself pleasing to Him. It is precisely what He wants us to occupy our time here on this earth doing. It is not merely a good habit. It will literally determine what kind of person you become. Our search builds up our Christian character, edifying us so that we can lead moral and holy lives that will in turn lead others to Christ.

From the days of the Old Testament, pious men knew how important it was to center their entire lives on finding God. The great prophet Isaiah wrote: "Seek the LORD while He may be found; Call upon Him while He is near. Let the wicked forsake his way, And the unrighteous man his thoughts; And let him return to the LORD, And He will have compassion on him, And to our God, For He will abundantly pardon" Isaiah 55:6–7 (KJV).

The choice is yours, as this scripture makes so plainly clear. To ignore God and forsake His ways—to wantonly ignore His laws and commandments, and to close your ears to His holy teachings—is accounted as wickedness. You can't simply say, "I don't care" and be indifferent when it comes to God! Yet, in the very next verse, we read about the Lord's compassion and forgiveness. All that is required is to "return to the Lord," which is, of course, at the heart of seeking God in the first place.

The most well-known and relevant Bible verse on this topic, not surprisingly, comes from none other than Jesus Himself, who explained it very succinctly in Matthew 7:7 (NIV), saying: "Ask, and it will be given to you; seek, and you will find; knock, and it will be opened to you. For everyone who asks receives, and he who seeks finds, and to him who knocks it will be opened."

Our Lord always knows how to get straight to the heart of the matter, doesn't He? Jesus tells us precisely what we must do. *Seek and you will find.* God is indeed omnipresent ... yet you will never find Him without seeking Him. Sure He could just appear right before your eyes, but He does not do that for a very good reason: there are so many invaluable lessons for us to learn from the process of seeking God! In His unfathomable wisdom, God has put in place all the clues we need for finding Him, but He leaves it up to us to discover those clues and put them all together. God is not going to do it for us. After all, how could a student learn anything if the teacher did all the work for him or her? No, a good teacher (and Jesus is the best!) equips the students with all that they need to figure out the answers for themselves.

Remember, never get frustrated as you seek God. Instead, go about your quest empowered by the Holy Spirit in the way that God intended for you to go about it. God said to the prophet Jeremiah, "You will seek Me and find Me when you search for Me with all your heart" Jeremiah 29:13 (NIV). So, this is not some kind of a one-shot deal. It is a way of life and a lifetime commitment. But the joyful benefits of seeking God are eternal in nature, and the wise man or woman realizes that the result of all their seeking is worth far more than any amount of effort they put into it.

Courage

Courage is the power of the mind to face difficulty. Examine yourself to discover what's difficult for you. Ask God to strengthen you to overcome that difficulty and give you the ability to be victorious when it comes to the obstacles in your life.

For example: if you can't read, ask God to help you learn to read and find someone to help you practice reading. If you're an addict, ask God to deliver you from your addiction and find someone to help you practice sobriety. If you're a liar, ask God to help you stop lying and find someone to help you practice stop lying and to be a more honest person. If you want more faith in confessing with your mouth that Jesus is Lord and believing in your heart that God raised Him from the dead, so you shall be saved (the gospel), then ask God to help you believe. Find someone—a mature, devout Christian—to help you practice believing the gospel.

Try this if you're really having trouble believing the gospel and fully embracing God's revelation to mankind. This exercise is for adult-use only. Light a candle and place your hand over the flame until it burns you. Ask yourself: "How many times am I willing to do this until I believe the flame burns me?" When you trust that placing your hand over the flame will burn you, now you have faith and will not do it again. Now you have faith that the candle will burn you, and therefore you will not place your hand over the candle again. When God helps you trust His word, you have faith. Believing and trusting are the same. If you modify your behavior to act according to the word, then that clearly demonstrates that you have faith that pleases God.

When you ask God for something, expect Him to answer your prayer and do something according to His will in that line.

The Bible says faith without works is dead. As you overcome your difficulties your courage increases, and you operate in victory. Always remember to thank God for your blessing.

The Bible teaches us many lessons about courage. In fact, God not only tells us to be courageous, He also *commands* it! Here is what we read in Joshua 1:9 (NIV)… "Have not I commanded thee? Be strong and of a good courage; be not afraid, neither be thou dismayed: for the LORD thy God is with thee whithersoever thou goest."

Notice, however, the powerful reason why God gives this remarkable admonition. He promises to be with us wherever we go. Therefore, we most certainly should be emboldened wherever we go and whatever we do, because we know that He is with us. It is the exact same promise that Jesus made before departing this Earth. In Matthew 28:20 (NIV), He said, "And surely, I am with you always, to the very end of the age."

If you know for sure that God quite literally has your back in any given situation or scenario, no matter how dangerous or precarious, do you really have anything to fear? Not if your faith is strong enough, for by faith we must believe exactly what it is that God is telling us: that He will always be right there with us, amidst every possible kind of adversity.

Do you recall the story of the fiery furnace? We find it in the Daniel 3:1-30 (NIV):

King Nebuchadnezzar built a gold statue, ninety feet high and nine feet thick. He set it up on the Dura plain in the province of Babylon. He then ordered all the important leaders in the province, everybody who was anybody, to the dedication ceremony of the statue. They all came for the dedication, all the important

people, and took their places before the statue that Nebuchadnezzar had erected.

4-6 A herald then proclaimed in a loud voice: "Attention, everyone! Every race, color, and creed, listen! When you hear the band strike up—all the trumpets and trombones, the tubas and baritones, the drums and cymbals—fall to your knees and worship the gold statue that King Nebuchadnezzar has set up. Anyone who does not kneel and worship shall be thrown immediately into a roaring furnace."

7 The band started to play, a huge band equipped with all the musical instruments of Babylon, and everyone—every race, color, and creed—fell to their knees and worshiped the gold statue that King Nebuchadnezzar had set up.

8-12 Just then, some Babylonian fortunetellers stepped up and accused the Jews. They said to King Nebuchadnezzar, "Long live the king! You gave strict orders, O king, that when the big band started playing, everyone had to fall to their knees and worship the gold statue, and whoever did not go to their knees and worship it had to be pitched into a roaring furnace. Well, there are some Jews here—Shadrach, Meshach, and Abednego—whom you have placed in high positions in the province of Babylon. These men are ignoring you, O king. They don't respect your gods and they won't worship the gold statue you set up."

13-15 Furious, King Nebuchadnezzar ordered Shadrach, Meshach, and Abednego to be brought in. When the men were brought in, Nebuchadnezzar asked, "Is it true, Shadrach, Meshach, and Abednego, that you don't respect my gods and refuse to worship the gold statue that I have set up? I'm giving you a second chance—but from now on, when the big band strikes up you must go to your knees and worship the statue I have made. If you don't worship it, you will be pitched into a roaring furnace, no questions asked. Who is the god who can rescue you from my power?"

16-18 Shadrach, Meshach, and Abednego answered King Nebuchadnezzar, "Your threat means nothing to us. If you throw us in the fire, the God we serve can rescue us from your roaring furnace and anything else you might cook up, O king. But even if he doesn't, it wouldn't make a bit of difference, O king. We still wouldn't serve your gods or worship the gold statue you set up."

19-23 Nebuchadnezzar, his face purple with anger, cut off Shadrach, Meshach, and Abednego. He ordered the furnace fired up seven times hotter than usual. He ordered some strong men from the army to tie them up, hands and feet, and throw them into the roaring furnace. Shadrach, Meshach, and Abednego, bound hand and foot, fully dressed from head to toe, were pitched into the roaring fire. Because the king was in such a hurry and the furnace was so hot, flames from the furnace killed the men who carried Shadrach,

Meshach, and Abednego to it, while the fire raged around Shadrach, Meshach, and Abednego.

[24] Suddenly King Nebuchadnezzar jumped up in alarm and said, "Didn't we throw three men, bound hand and foot, into the fire?"

"That's right, O king," they said.

[25] "But look!" he said. "I see four men, walking around freely in the fire, completely unharmed! And the fourth man looks like a son of the gods!"

[26] Nebuchadnezzar went to the door of the roaring furnace and called in, "Shadrach, Meshach, and Abednego, servants of the High God, come out here!"

Shadrach, Meshach, and Abednego walked out of the fire.

[27] All the important people, the government leaders and king's counselors, gathered around to examine them and discovered that the fire hadn't so much as touched the three men—not a hair singed, not a scorch mark on their clothes, not even the smell of fire on them!

[28] Nebuchadnezzar said, "Blessed be the God of Shadrach, Meshach, and Abednego! He sent his angel and rescued his servants who trusted in him! They ignored the king's orders and laid their bodies

on the line rather than serve or worship any god but their own.

²⁹ "Therefore I issue this decree: Anyone anywhere, of any race, color, or creed, who says anything against the God of Shadrach, Meshach, and Abednego will be ripped to pieces, limb from limb, and their houses torn down. There has never been a god who can pull off a rescue like this."

³⁰ Then the king promoted Shadrach, Meshach, and Abednego in the province of Babylon.

Take a moment and think about the incredible story that you just read. Now ask yourself: how in the world did those three youths find the courage to defy the king and be willing to succumb to such a horrible death? The answer is right in the story itself: "But look!" he said. "I see four men, walking around freely in the fire, completely unharmed! And the fourth man looks like a son of the gods!" Yes, that "fourth man" was indeed Jesus Christ Himself. In other words, God was right there with Shadrach, Meshach, and Abednego, giving all three of them the courage to faithfully follow Him.

OK, you may ask: but where exactly does such courage come from for me? I'm no hero. I'm not Rambo out on some battlefield someplace, I'm just a regular, everyday person. Well, no problem! The source of all courage for each and every one of us today as well as in Bible times remains unchanged: it is still none other than God Himself. The holy scriptures make this abundantly clear throughout both the Old and New Testament, but for our purposes here we will use just two very illustrative examples.

First, consider Psalm 27:1(NIV): "The LORD is my light and my salvation—whom shall I fear? The LORD is the stronghold of my life—of whom shall I be afraid?" This is the ultimate reason why the man or woman who trusts in God should always live with courage. You know that His light will show you the way, and His power inevitably leads to salvation. Therefore, fear flees from your heart when you come to the stark realization: *Why am I afraid? Don't I trust God?*

And that's the pivotal question, isn't it, because, as always it comes down to a matter of faith.

Finally in the New Testament, we read the unforgettable words of Jesus Himself: "Peace I leave with you; my peace I give you. I do not give to you as the world gives. Do not let your hearts be troubled and do not be afraid" John 14:27 (NIV).

What an incredible encouragement this is, directly from the lips of our Lord and Savior! It makes us view the whole idea of courage in an entirely different light. The world thinks in terms of physical bravery. People admire and often are in awe of "tough guys" who will not flinch when it comes to going toe to toe with any opponent. Other times we see the physical courage of those who would risk their own life to save others, such as running into a burning building to rescue people.

However, though there is certainly value in those qualities, Jesus is teaching us about something quite different. He is telling us that we can have the courage ("Do not be afraid") to find true peace ("Do not let your hearts be troubled") even in our violent, often seemingly crazy world because, as Jesus tells us in John 16:33 (NIV), He has "overcome the world." That means if we follow Him with genuine Christian courage, we can overcome the world, too.

Discipline

Discipline is training to act in accordance with rules. There are rules that cover every area of our existence. We have rules to stay alive. If we break them we die. We have rules to perform our chosen professions. If we break those we're fired or suffer other losses. We have rules to become children of God. We must confess with our mouth that Jesus is Lord and believe in our hearts that God raised Him from the dead to be saved. If we break that one we're eternally separated from God. As you can see, when we modify our behavior to comply with rules there are benefits. We become children of God. No other accolades are better.

But what do we need to do, as Christians, to bring discipline into our lives? Recognize first that we can always choose to maintain discipline. Although years of bad habits can make us think about doing things the wrong way—breaking the rules—we know in our hearts when we have gone astray. That inborn tendency to stray away from righteousness is part of the human condition, our fallen human nature, and this internal battle is a lifelong struggle. Yet through grace we can find victory in our lives.

So what exactly is happening when we find it so hard to do what we innately know is right? The answer is: our old sinful nature is fighting for control. When we become Christians, we renounce our old sinful nature and let Jesus have the final say over every area of our life. Discipline plays such a key and vital role in this, making sure that regardless of what our old habits or the world or our culture is telling us to do, we make the decision that honors Jesus instead. Apostle Paul said in Romans 7: 19 (NIV), "For I do not do the good I want to do, but the evil I do not want to do—this I keep on doing." You see, even this holy man who had a supernatural encounter with Jesus Christ on the road to Damascus, and who wrote much of the New Testament, had difficulty maintaining discipline. It wasn't that he didn't know the difference between right and wrong—and he acknowledges he wanted to choose what was right—but he felt like he kept getting pulled in the opposite direction. But Paul also reveals how he was able to choose to do what was right; it was not in his own power but in his dependence on the power of God that he was able to win his battle with his sinful nature. In Romans 7:25 (NIV) Paul wrote "Thanks be to God, who delivers me through Jesus Christ our Lord!" Paul was able to stay on course and maintain his discipline only because God helped him win his daily battle.

Listening to Paul's heartfelt words, we can all empathize with him because we all face the very same challenge that he did. It is indeed humbling to admit such shortcomings. But Paul is also our witness that we can be victorious in our fight to live a disciplined life.

The Bible says we must "die to self." Now that's discipline! It requires us to take the backseat while handing over control to Jesus. We must follow a sense of duty, as would a good and loyal soldier. Maintaining such discipline means studying God's word as much as possible, in fact so much so that His ways start to instinctively become our ways. This requires daily prayer, hiding the Word deep within your heart so that when temptation comes along urging you to go astray, you have cultivated the necessary self-discipline to exercise proper self-control. That is the most reliable method of keeping ourselves on the "narrow road" that Jesus assured us leads to eternal life.

Honesty

Honesty is the quality of being honest. Quality is a degree or grade of excellence, and honesty is being honorable in principles and actions. We are all God's people and He made us in His image. We are empowered to choose to be honest. If you honestly apply these principles outlined and discussed in this book, you will change for the better. Therefore honestly identify events, thoughts, feelings, fantasies, and urges to align them to the principles outlined in this book. The better you know yourself, the more empowered you will be to keep or discard behaviors and choose rules that build you up instead of tearing you down.

Let's consider a recent event that an addict testified to at an Alcoholics Anonymous meeting. She had gone a number of months through pregnancy and the birth of her child without using drugs. She was now, however, experiencing urges to use drugs. This young woman came to the meeting seeking answers on how to maintain her sobriety. Her major challenge was not to give in to using drugs. All God's people are born with an evil nature that craves to do evil, yet (thank you, Father!) He empowered us all to choose to stay free from sin. He fashioned our bodies to signal us to resist feelings and thoughts to repeat behaviors that cause guilt, shame, remorse, unhealthy anger, and anxiety. The signals that go with these thoughts and feelings are wandering minds, burden, sweaty palms, racing heartbeats, etc. When signals occur, recognize what you're thinking and feeling, and purge yourself of all negative thoughts right away. This is what the new mother did when she came to the AA meeting seeking help to avoid using drugs.

I also explained to her that although I'm unable to imagine what she's experiencing, I am able to note a few facts per her testimony. She had gone eleven months free of drugs because she valued protecting her baby from the destructive effects of narcotics. God gave her the power to resist her old bad habits that long. Now He directed her steps to this meeting tonight to receive this message. God empowers with signals that alert us of problems coming or at hand, He empowers us to choose the right path, and makes available principles to live by. Pay close attention to what you're feeling and thinking and choose, no matter what, to be loyal to the principles listed in this book.

Let me also add that without honesty, none of this is possible. In Proverbs 10:9 (NIV) we read: "Whoever walks in integrity walks securely, but whoever walks in crooked paths will be found out." The words "crooked paths" are synonymous with dishonesty, and the Lord is here teaching us that when we are dishonest, to our great shame the truth will ultimately be revealed. That is what the scripture means when it says, "God is not mocked." Those things that are done "in the darkness" (i.e., dishonestly) will inevitably be unveiled by the inescapable light of God's truth.

Those who fail to live their lives honestly may get away with it for a while, but in the end they are only fooling themselves. God not only loves honesty, He requires it. It is, after all, one of the Ten Commandments ("Thou shalt not bear false witness"). God Himself, of course, has absolutely no falsehood in Him. None. He is teaching His children to set their sights high, with the goal and objective of being just like Him. That is why, in Matthew 5:48 (NIV), Jesus said, "Be perfect, therefore, as your heavenly Father is perfect."

The opposite is the devil. Here is what Jesus said about those who by their own free will follow him: "You belong to your father, the devil, and you want to carry out your father's desires.

He was a murderer from the beginning, not holding to the truth, for there is no truth in him. When he lies, he speaks his native language, for he is a liar and the father of lies" John 8:44 (NIV).

Could the contrast be any stronger? Choose to live in honesty and integrity. Choose to live God's way.

Respect

Respect is acknowledging (honoring or esteeming) the rights, privileges, and positions of another. God's people fall tremendously in this area. They don't respect God, others, or themselves. That is why this book is so important. It reminds people of what must be done to show respect. The addicts and stiff-necked are stuck in a rut. They must choose to break free of their problems, and be willing to benefit in the blessings of respecting God and the laws of the land.

One individual testified that he didn't respect God, himself, and others each time he used drugs and got drunk. He would use his drugs of choice, go to a bar, drink until he blacked out, fight, drive God knows where, and wake up in the morning having no clue what happened the day before. Another individual testified that day after day he would drink, pray, and pass out. He was unsatisfied about drinking and couldn't stop. In each case they believed they had no choice but to use their drugs of choice. Also, in each case they wanted help. One was forced into a rehab center and the other came to an AA meeting, chose a sponsor, worked the twelve steps, prayed the serenity prayer, and both have been sober over twenty years. Both still pray and thank God for their sobriety but claim they're still alcoholics.

I also know how much I value my freedom and how much I value being with my wife. But God allowed me to be arrested and imprisoned for motor fuel taxes. My prayer was to deliver me, set me free, and bless me with fifty thousand five hundred dollars a day for each case filed against me. Then I forgave everyone who had done me wrong. I respected God when I humbled myself to His will with the right attitude, and committed myself to what He wanted me to learn and do for Him. The benefits of respecting God is knowing I'm a child of God, He protected me the entire time in a dangerous prison for three years, and He's trusting me to oversee the Holy Temple of God and its outreach faith-based program.

The Lord also enables me to express my love to Him and His people by obeying His will by teaching His people the principles outlined in this book and following His leadership and guidance in developing the Holy Temple of God and His faith-based program.

Before incarceration, *I trusted and obeyed God's counsel, leadership, and guidance over my life. But during and after incarceration, God has blessed me with a sensitivity to His will that causes me to think less evil (sin). I'm practicing to get through one day at a time without thinking sin. I respect Him so much for how close we've become.* Our closeness enables me to honor and esteem God for who He is. I am able to honor and esteem HIM FOR WHO He is because He has blessed me in very special ways.

One day while in my field cutting grass, a rain shower abruptly appeared. I burst out in pleading to take the rain away. Almost instantly the rain stopped, the sun appeared, and I was able to complete my chore. On another occasion, I was in praise and worship service after cutting the flesh on my finger with a pressure washer water blast, all the way down to the white meat just shy of the bone. As I worshipped, the sting would interfere with concentrating on the Lord. I cried out that the pain be taken away. Like a dog licking my finger the pain was licked away.

Later in testimony service, I was able to tell what God had done for me. While incarcerated and before getting out to search for an attorney to defend me in court (which I couldn't afford), I was praying in my jail cell about something I can't remember. *I felt wetness on my forehead as of an impression of a cross. The Lord blessed my heart to understand that someone was praying for me. This occurred on a Tuesday night. The next opportunity to speak with my wife, I asked her if she was praying for me the last Tuesday night. She stated that she prays for me all the time. I shared my experience with her about that Tuesday night. I got out on bail to search for an attorney and went to church and asked the elders. They also stated that they pray for me all the time but couldn't identify with my experience of my forehead being anointed with oil. Immediately after conversations with them, the Pastor walked into the sanctuary. It was like an obsession to know who had prayed for me and asked God to do this wonderful thing for me. Without even greeting her, I asked her if she prayed for me on a Tuesday night. She threw her hands up in praise to the Lord and testified that on a recent Tuesday night, she anointed her head or the air with blessing oil and asked God to dispatch His angel to deliver this anointing on me. Oh, we had a glorious time in the Lord that night!*

The Bible has much to teach us about respect: for God, for others, and for ourselves. First, when it comes to God, the Bible uses the word "fear," saying in Ecclesiastes 12:13 (NIV) that we should "fear God". This has everything to do with being afraid of Him. Fearing God is about a profound sense of respect as we stand in reverence and in awe of His boundless majesty. Knowing this, and practicing it, is what makes you truly wise.

That is why we read in Proverbs 9:10 (NIV) that "the fear of the Lord is the beginning of wisdom." All other learning, everything that can possibly enlighten your mind, has to start from that basic premise.

When it comes to respecting other people, the greatest lesson Jesus taught us comes from the Sermon on the Mount. In Matthew 5:43–48 (NIV), we read:

> [43] "You have heard that it was said, 'You shall love your neighbor and hate your enemy.' [44] But I say to you, Love your enemies and pray for those who persecute you, [45] so that you may be sons of your Father who is in heaven. For he makes his sun rise on the evil and on the good, and sends rain on the just and on the unjust. [46] For if you love those who love you, what reward do you have? Do not even the tax collectors do the same? [47] And if you greet only your brothers,[a] what more are you doing than others? Do not even the Gentiles do the same? [48] You therefore must be perfect, as your heavenly Father is perfect.

Wow! That is so counterintuitive to our human minds and to the world's way of looking at things. Love our enemies? Yes! If we realize that even those we oppose are nonetheless made in the image of God, we will then respect them to the point where we learn to not only tolerate them but to love them. It involves, as Jesus said, being "perfect" which of course, by ourselves in our fallen state, is not possible, but with God's help all things are possible and we can indeed learn to love as He loves. Unconditionally.

Finally, in addition to respecting God and respecting other

people, we must have self-respect as well. One great example comes from Galatians 2:20 (NIV), where it says, "I have died, but Christ lives in me. And I now live by faith in the Son of God, who loved me and gave his life for me."

When you realize that Christ lives on the inside of you, it becomes clear that you are a saved, sanctified individual of such great worth that God was willing to sacrifice His only begotten Son for you. Therefore, if God so highly values you, the least you can do is to be sure to live in such a way that you respect yourself for who you are and live accordingly by leading a Godly life and always being careful that you never bring shame to God or to yourself by your actions, but instead bring glory to God our Father.

Responsibility

Responsibilities are simply good duties that are assigned or agreed upon. Sometimes people get confused about what they're really responsible for doing in his or her life. Rest assured that it is never your responsibility or duty to knowingly do something (anything) that you clearly recognize as wrong—regardless of who is asking you to do it, for such a request will never come from God, nor would it ever be pleasing to Him.

Are you a responsible person? I'm not talking about just one area of your life but in all areas of your life. God gives us a whole host of duties. He also gives you gifts to complete your tasks. That's why Bible studies, Sunday school, and a formal education are so important, so we can be successful in completing the duties God assign us. Don't get discouraged when anyone falsely accuses and wrongly does things to you. Just stand firmly in the truth and God will strengthen you to journey through your trials. Are you fulfilling your duties of being prosperous, being in good health, and being spiritually mature? Throughout my life I have had a strong sense of duty to help anyone in need. Sometimes these people take my kindness for weakness and take advantage of my good deeds. As a Christian you are strong, and your kindness is in fact the precise opposite of weakness. It is instead an indicator of your strength.

Be very careful not to add duties that you shouldn't or can't perform. Placing yourself in that position can lead to bad decisions to perform tasks that are risky, unsafe, or sinful. God and man assign duties. In all instances we are required to obey God's duties rather than man's duties, but in some instances we are not required to obey man's duties. We are not required to obey man's duties if they're requiring us to disobey God's duties. We can find everything we're responsible for in the Holy Scriptures. Just because you may not believe this determination doesn't relieve you of your duties. From the beginning we have a holy duty to obey God first, and also to obey lawful authority here on earth. In obedience, we express our love to God. As you can see, we have responsibilities that must be performed whether we agree with them or not. Remaining forever obedient to God and always doing what is righteous is what truly counts.

Tolerance

Tolerance is a virtue that enables you to have a fair and objective attitude toward anyone whose opinions about anything differ from your own view. This virtue is where one can bring together all the principles mentioned in this book to work for you. When situations arise, you will have a proven number of principles to work with to successfully complete your agreed-upon or assigned task. Although you may not agree on a responsibility assigned to you, you will nonetheless have or seek out the correct course to successfully complete your task. A tolerant person has the requisite humility to know that he or she is not always right, along with respect for those with whom we may not see eye to eye, always treating them properly and with dignity.

REPENT(ANCE)

To repent is to feel guilt, shame, remorse, anger, and anxiety; and to turn from sin to God. Without feeling terrible about wrong actions and turning from them, you have not truly repented.

It's so important that you understand how this beautiful redemptive process works, for it is indeed the heart and soul of Christianity. In fact, according to Matthew 4:17 (NIV), from the beginning of His ministry Jesus proclaimed, "Repent, for the kingdom of God has come near." In other words, with the arrival of Jesus, mankind was given an unprecedented opportunity to repent. That means we can come to Jesus so that that we can turn our lives around. Rather than being slaves to sin as we once were as fallen human beings, we are now free in Christ, fully forgiven for all our transgressions. They have been "washed white as snow" through the precious shed blood of our Savior.

When you repent, it is not merely saying some special words as if it's a magic formula. No, it's so much more than that. It's literally turning your life around. You are no longer living for yourself (i.e., sinfully) but, once you have been born again, you are living for God. It is not your own will that rules your life anymore, it is God calling the shots, through the Holy Spirit living on the inside of you now as a Christian. That is the key to genuine repentance.

Moreover, this repentance is for the entire world. It says in Acts 20:21 (NIV), "I have declared to both Jews and Greeks that they must turn to God in repentance and have faith in our Lord Jesus." When you firmly trust in Him, repentance comes full circle. Not only are you forgiven of your sins, but in your new repentant state of being you are empowered and energized to lead others to Christ, as you help fulfill the Great Commission of spreading the Gospel starting from Jerusalem (the Jewish people), out to the Greek culture and ultimately to the entire world, i.e., all humanity.

FORGIVE(NESS)

To forgive means to grant a pardon for a past debt. Search for past actions that you have thought or acted out and ask God to bless you to feel burdened by them and ask Him to forgive you. He is just and kind and will forgive you. Remember to trust that He has forgiven you and don't try to forgive yourself. If you can forgive yourself, you don't need God to forgive you. As surely as you trust the gospel of Jesus Christ, you must trust everything God says in scripture including repent. When you truly repent, God will forgive you. **He promised in 2 Chronicles 7:14 (NIV) that if my people, who are called by my name, will humble themselves and pray and seek my face and turn from their wicked ways, then I will hear from heaven, and I will forgive their sins and will heal their land.** You can trust Him as surely as you know that fire will burn you.

God's forgiveness also has amazing implications for our everyday lives. Not only do we read in the Lord's Prayer, "Forgive us our trespasses as we forgive those who trespass against us," but it also further says in Colossians 3:13 (NIV), "Bear with each other and forgive one another if any of you has a grievance against someone. Forgive as the Lord forgave you."

Remember, Jesus even forgave those who crucified Him! Therefore, if He could show that much mercy, how hard is it for us to forgive friends, family, even strangers when we feel some-one has done something wrong to us? If we really want to imitate Jesus and conform ourselves to His character, we need to learn to have a forgiving heart just as Jesus does. Don't let the sun go down with bitterness still festering in your heart. It will destroy you from the inside out. Instead, keep in mind the venerable old saying, "To err is human, to forgive is divine." And then live accordingly.

Trust and Obey God

Trusting and obeying are essential elements of pleasing and loving God. The scripture says Abraham pleased God when he believed Him. And God also said in John 14:15 (KJV), "Why do you say you love me when you don't obey Me." As you can see we must trust Him and obey his every word.

On a day-to-day basis, what can we do to show God that we trust Him and want to obey Him? It all has to do with how we go about living our everyday lives. I think Psalm 13:5 (NIV) expresses it beautifully: "But I trust in your unfailing love; my heart rejoices in your salvation."

When you have that kind of faith in God, it changes your entire outlook on life. You are trusting that God's love will never fail. That means you acknowledge that He is your Father, He loves you more than you could ever imagine, and therefore you are joyful. As the verse says, your heart rejoices in (God's) salvation.

That joy is contagious! Others will not only recognize it, they will be touched by it. The Kingdom of God will be built up one soul at a time as people throughout the world stop trusting in their own wisdom, and instead put all their hopes and dreams in the one place they can completely trust—into the hands of God. We must vow, with absolute trust as Jesus did as He died upon the Cross: "Father, into thine hands I commend my spirit" Luke 23:46 (KJV)!

SUMMARY

As we've now seen, the purpose of the Principles of Life Outreach Program is to share tangible leadership and guidance you must use especially when confronted with situations and circumstances that may cause you to choose the easy way out. The easy way out always makes you vulnerable to grief, shame, hurt, and despair. Although these rules alone do not ensure that you obey these principles, you must trust God's Word. This entire book is based on God's word. They are my lifestyle choices that strengthened me to journey through technical training, a master's program, a military career, management experience, and even prison while reaching out to people everywhere in love.

The principles shared here are focus, humility, prayer, seeking God, repentance, forgiveness, and trusting and obeying God's word. If you are loyal to these principles, you will change for the good and can be trusted to do great things for the Lord. Remember: there is a difference between saved and unsaved, honesty and dishonesty, and repentance and lip service. I beg you not to fall into a trap. These principles work only *if you work them*. Remember: faith without works is dead and works without faith is dead.

Holy Temple of God's Principles of Life Outreach Program

Mission Statement

Our mission is to provide everyone this set of principles that empowers you to not choose the easy way out. Being loyal to these principles will enable you to make the right choices in all situations and circumstances. Sometimes you will be misunderstood, lied to, persecuted, or in extreme cases, even killed. Nevertheless, always remain steadfastly obedient to these principles and God assures you will have a better life ahead despite your experiences, if not in this world then most assuredly in the life of the world to come.

Founded

The Holy Temple of God and its faith-based program was founded in 2007 while I was in prison serving time for allegedly stealing motor fuel taxes. I served three years and was released on parole in February 2009. I continue to express my love to God and His people through obedience, thankfulness, and my deeds according to His will for none to perish.

Teaching Guide

The Holy Temple of God's Faith-Based Program utilizes this book as a teaching guide for all students who apply and are chosen to attend this program. Upon completion, all students will be offered employment in Travis Roberson's Limited Liability Company (LLC) at a minimum wage of twelve dollars an hour. All employees of Travis Roberson's LLC must graduate from the Holy Temple of God's Faith-Based Program.

Thank you for reading, and may God richly bless you.

CPSIA information can be obtained
at www.ICGtesting.com
Printed in the USA
LVHW09*2034081018
R14008500001B/R140085PG591806LVX1B/2/P

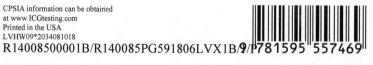